The Women's Institute

vintage teatime

SIMON & SCHUSTER ILLUSTRATED

London · New York · Sydney · Toronto · New Delhi

A CBS COMPANY

Compiled by **Jessica Simmons**

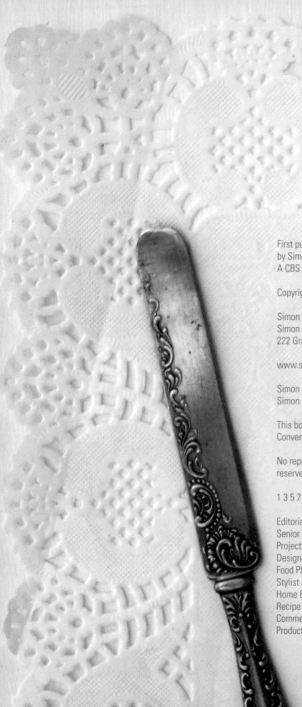

First published in Great Britain
by Simon & Schuster UK Ltd, 2012
A CBS Company

Simon & Schuster Illustrated Books,
Simon & Schuster UK Ltd
222 Gray's Inn Road, London WC1X 8HB

www.simonandschuster.co.uk

Simon & Schuster Australia, Sydney
Simon & Schuster India, New Delhi

1 3 5 7 9 10 8 6 4 2

Editorial Director: **Francine Lawrence**
Senior Commissioning Editor: **Nicky Hill**
Project Editor: **Nicki Lampon**
Designer: **Richard Proctor**
Food Photographer: **William Shaw**
Stylist and Art Direction: **Tony Hutchinson**
Home Economist: **Sara Lewis**
Recipe Consultant: **Sîan Cook**
Commercial Director: **Ami Richards**
Production Manager: **Katherine Thornton**

Colour reproduction by Dot Gradations Ltd, UK.
Printed and bound in China.

A CIP catalogue for this book is available from the
British Library.

ISBN 978-0-85720-859-0

Notes on the recipes
Both metric and imperial measurements have
been given in all recipes. Use one set of
measurements only and not a mixture of both.
Spoon measures are level and 1 tablespoon =
15 ml, 1 teaspoon = 5 ml.

Preheat ovens before use and cook on the centre
shelf unless cooking more than one item. If using
a fan oven, reduce the heat by 10–20°C, but
check with your handbook.

Medium eggs have been used unless otherwise
stated.

This book contains recipes made with nuts.
Those with known allergic reactions to nuts
and nut derivatives, pregnant and breast-feeding
women and very young children should avoid
these dishes.

We endeavoured to source recipes and seek
permission from as many federations as possible,
however we sadly haven't had room to represent
each one. With thanks to those who gave advice
and support in the research of the book.

Contents

Introduction

Whether you're sipping piping hot tea served from a china tea cup between considered rounds of crustless sandwiches; spreading a warm, home-made scone with fresh clotted cream and jam or simply deliberating over a delicately stacked pile of pastries and cakes, it's hard to deny the quintessentially British culinary experience that is afternoon tea.

First thought to have been taken by Anna Russell, 7th Duchess of Bedford (and a good friend of Queen Victoria) around 1840, a modest late-afternoon snack of bread and butter evolved into a handsome spread of finger sandwiches and dainty cakes washed down with tea – the perfect excuse for a new wave of refined social gatherings in 19th-century Britain.

Afternoon tea and the WI

In 1915 a pioneering women's organisation that was to become synonymous with domestic excellence in home cooking and baking was borne – The Women's Institute. Never an organisation to shy away from duty in a time of national crisis, many members became heavily involved in the wartime production of jam and trained as rural food leaders in their communities, campaigning on a range of topical food issues through national resolutions. Yet it was their hearty spread of hand-crafted loaves, cakes, buns and pastries, showcased to the public via market stalls and show tents, that earned the WI its life-long medal of distinction for home-baked goods during the decades to follow.

The 'art' of afternoon tea
Fast forward to the hectic lifestyles and stresses of 21st century living, and it's no surprise that home baking, the Women's Institute and the 'art' of afternoon tea are experiencing a welcome resurgence in popularity. Afternoon tea has become a lavish affair and a coveted diary date, easily replacing lunch, dinner or both as the lost art of conversation is re-discovered amid pots of tea and cucumber sandwiches.

Classic recipes from the WI archives
This classic collection of authentic, tried and trusted recipes is taken from the archives of the Women's Institute; a comprehensive menu of old-fashioned teatime treats to enable you to host your own vintage afternoon tea party. Recipes date back as far as 1930 and highlight the wealth of domestic knowledge from individual WI members who contributed their best recipes, tips and advice as part of their WI Federation recipe books. Loosely based on counties, there are currently 69 WI Federations in England, Wales and the islands that fall under the National Federation of Women's Institutes (NFWI). Many of the recipe books' front covers are emblazoned with delightful illustrations and timeless fonts, offering a nod to the appropriate decade of publication, while inside lie nostalgic favourites such as Yorkshire Fat Rascals (page 82), Dorset Apple Cake (page 85), Wiltshire Lardy Cake (page 90) and Devonshire Splits (page 86) to name but a few. Each Federation is rightfully proud of its culinary heritage, often summarised in a heart-felt foreword from the WI Federation chairman of the time. We've endeavoured to include some of the best snippets with the recipes. Each cake, biscuit, pastry or savoury has its own story to tell.

An interesting take on regional specialities appears in *Traditional Fare of England and Wales* published by the NFWI in 1948 (it sold for two shillings and sixpence). While it was noted that the collected recipes would 'keep on record the traditional art of the English housewife', a J.M. Winnington told readers in the book's introduction that: 'It is mis-leading, except in a few particular instances, to attach place names to recipes for owing to the migration of populations in times of depression, the same methods recur in different parts of the country.' While we'd surely defend the Devonshire Split's geographical title rights as a means of identifying the breadth of British cuisine, it's indeed a fact that, across a comprehensive range of WI recipe books, the 'classic' cakes, pastries and biscuits can moonlight under various guises, ingredients listings and methods of baking. No less than four versions of Ginger Crunchies (page 110) appear in Norfolk Federation's *More Good Recipes* (1957) – these ask for a cool oven, a moderate oven (two recipes) and a fairly hot oven in their respective baking requirements. Such was the range cooker's simplicity at this time, temperature guestimates might have been a risky business for kitchen novices. We have made slight adjustments to some recipes, where necessary, so that some of the older methods of weighing, preparing and cooking ingredients, are in line with today's modern appliances.

Vintage teatime

WI *Vintage Teatime* is a collection of cherished recipes that, through the WI archives, celebrates domesticity and shared knowledge at its best between generations of home cooks and bakers. But before we tie our apron strings and begin baking we might also look to a poetic recipe for 'The Cake of Happiness', which consists of 'a pound of belief in providence, a pint of tenderness, a cupful of confidence', and not forgetting to 'sweeten with cheerfulness' – a seemingly fitting ode to the joy of baking from WI member Mrs Dawson of Old Costessy in the aforementioned *More Good Recipes*.

All you need now are some pretty cups, saucers and plates, a good cake knife and a few of your favourite people. For a special occasion with a vintage twist why not light up the table with a delicious cherry and almond Meringue-Topped Cake (page 49), Golden Layer Cake (page 50) or choux pastry Party Rings (page 46) filled with fresh cream and peaches? Whether you're hosting your own afternoon tea from the comfort of your home, indulging in a comforting teatime snack of Pikelets (page 72) and cake or throwing a regal-themed street party for your neighbours and friends, there's really never been a better excuse to make time for tea. HRH Queen Elizabeth, a long-standing member of the Women's Institute, would no doubt thoroughly approve.

For 30 cups of tea you will need:
40 g (1½ oz) tea
4½ litres (8 pints) water
1.2 litres (2 pints) milk
Taken from 1970s' leaflet *Let's Give a Party*, by Bookhams Evening WI, Surrey Federation of Women's Institutes.

Savoury teatime treats

Drop scones

These get their name from the fact that spoonfuls of the mixture are dropped on to a hot griddle to cook them.

Makes about 24
Preparation time:
 15 minutes
Cooking time:
 8–10 minutes

225 g (8 oz) **plain flour**
15 g (½ oz) **caster sugar**
a pinch of **salt**
1 teaspoon **baking powder**
1 **egg**
1 teaspoon **golden syrup**
250 ml (9 fl oz) **milk**

Sift the flour, sugar, salt and baking powder into a bowl. Beat together the egg and golden syrup in a large jug.

Add the milk to the egg and syrup and stir into the dry ingredients. The batter should be like a thick cream.

Drop dessertspoons of the mixture on to a hot griddle pan or frying pan and brown both sides, turning as soon as bubbles begin to form.

Tip Often served with butter and jam, these are delicious as a savoury snack with cream cheese, smoked salmon, diced hard-boiled egg and a little mustard and cress.

Walnut and raisin bread

This recipe featured in the WI magazine *Home & Country* in March 1969 and was described as a 'winner at the children's tea'.

Serves 8
Preparation time:
 20 minutes
Baking time:
 50–60 minutes

350 g (12 oz) **wholemeal flour**
4 teaspoons **baking powder**
½ teaspoon **salt**
60 g (2 oz) **white vegetable fat**
60 g (2 oz) **caster sugar**
60 g (2 oz) **raisins**
110 g (4 oz) **walnuts**, roughly chopped
1 large **egg**
300 ml (10 fl oz) **milk**

Grease a 450 g (1 lb) loaf tin and preheat the oven to 180°C/350°F/Gas Mark 4.

Sieve the flour, baking powder and salt together into a bowl. Rub the fat into the mixture. Add the sugar, raisins and walnuts.

Beat the egg and mix it into the dry ingredients with the milk. It will be a fairly slack mixture – too soft to handle.

Spoon the mixture into the tin and bake for 50–60 minutes. Cover the top with foil towards the end of the cooking time if the top seems to be browning too quickly. Make sure it is done by inserting a skewer into the centre – if it is cooked, it will come out clean.

Cool in the tin for a few minutes and then turn out on to a wire rack.

Barley bread

In Elizabethan England, barley bread was a common option for a thrifty supper. Serve warm with lashings of butter and jam.

Serves 6
Preparation time:
   10 minutes
Baking time:
   25–30 minutes

425 g (15 oz) **barley flour**
140 g (5 oz) **plain flour**
1 teaspoon **salt**
1 teaspoon **bicarbonate
   of soda**
2 teaspoons **cream of tartar**
60 ml (2 fl oz) **buttermilk**

Preheat the oven to 190°C/370°F/Gas Mark 5. Place a greased baking tray in the oven.

Mix the dry ingredients together and add most of the buttermilk until the mixture forms a dough (you may not need to use all the buttermilk).

Divide the mixture into two. Roll each half out on a lightly floured surface to a 2.5 cm (1 inch) thick round. Bake on the preheated baking tray for 25–30 minutes until golden brown and cooked through.

Tips Wholegrain spelt flour can be used instead of the barley flour.

This can also be cooked on a hot griddle, turning the rounds over when the underside is cooked.

Muffins

English muffins became particularly fashionable during the 18th century. Split and serve with butter for a lovely teatime treat.

Makes 24
Preparation time:
  30 minutes + about
  2 hours rising
Baking time:
  12–15 minutes

1.1 kg (2 lb 7 oz) **strong white bread flour**
2 teaspoons **caster sugar**
15 g (½ oz) **salt**
2½ teaspoons **fast action dried yeast**
plain flour and **semolina**, to coat

Place the flour in a large mixing bowl and stir in the sugar, salt and yeast. Make a well in the centre and pour in 600 ml (20 fl oz) of warm water. Mix to make a soft dough. Turn out on to an unfloured surface and knead for 8–10 minutes.

Place in a greased bowl and cover with oiled cling film. Set aside in a warm place to double in size for 1 hour.

Knock back, roll out to 5 mm (½ inch) thick and cut into rounds to make about 24 muffins. Place well apart on greased and floured baking trays, dust the tops with a mixture of flour and semolina and set aside in a warm place again until double in size. Preheat the oven to 220°C/425°C/Gas Mark 7.

Bake in the oven for 12–15 minutes until golden. Alternatively, cook on a greased griddle pan for about 7 minutes, cooking both sides evenly.

Notes From *More Yeast Cookery*. 'Good places to prove dough are on the rack over a stove, in the warming oven, in front of a fire or open oven door, or over a pan of warm water'.

'Bread can be set to prove three times, but the housewife usually proved bread twice, except when making "quick bread", which is only proved once.'

Potted meat

A myriad of on-the-shelf sandwich fillers have overtaken once-fashionable potted meat, but this version is all the better for being home-made.

Serves 8–10
Preparation time:
1 hour
Cooking time: 5 hours

450 g (1 lb) **lean stewing beef**
1 teaspoon coarsely crushed **black peppercorns**
½ teaspoon **salt**
1 **allspice berry**
½ **bay leaf**
1 **mace blade** or a good grating of fresh **nutmeg**
2 teaspoons **anchovy paste** or a small tin **anchovy fillets**, drained
60 g (2 oz) **butter**, plus 25–40 g (1–1½ oz) for sealing
a little chopped fresh **parsley**

Preheat the oven to 140°C/275°F/Gas Mark 1.

Wash and dry the beef and cut into small pieces, removing any fat and sinew. Put into a greased ovenproof dish with a tight-fitting lid. Add the seasoning, all the spices and herbs and the anchovy paste or fillets and dot with the butter. Cover with the lid.

Cook for 5 hours, stirring half way through the cooking time.

Either spoon the contents into a food processor, removing the bay leaf, and blend until smooth or, for a coarse texture, chop well with a knife and fork.

Divide between ramekin dishes or spoon into one large dish. Melt the extra butter (you will need the larger amount for the ramekins), combine with the parsley and spoon over the surface.

Tip Sealing with butter allows you to keep the potted meat for up to a week in the fridge.

Variation For added flavour, try adding a little garlic, chopped fresh rosemary, some of your favourite fresh herbs, or even a splash of sherry.

Mini sausage and egg pies

These delicious little pies are a variation on pork pies and should be made the day before they are eaten. The savoury jelly can be omitted if you wish.

Makes 4
Preparation time:
 30–40 minutes
Cooking time:
 30–35 minutes

2 **eggs**
250 g (9 oz) **puff pastry**,
 defrosted if frozen
400 g (14 oz) **pork sausage
 meat** or 6 **pork sausages**,
 skinned
½ teaspoon **mixed herbs**
½ teaspoon **Home-made
 mustard** (page 23)
salt and freshly ground
 black pepper
1 **egg**, beaten, to seal
 and glaze

Savoury jelly
140 ml (5 fl oz) **meat stock**
½ heaped tablespoon
 gelatine

To make the savoury jelly, put the meat stock and gelatine into a saucepan. Stir over a gentle heat until every grain of gelatine has disappeared. Season well. Use when the jelly is cool. You will only need some of the jelly. Preheat the oven to 200°C/400°F/Gas Mark 6.

Add the eggs to a small pan of water, bring to the boil and simmer for 6 minutes. Rinse with cold water and peel.

Cut the pastry into four pieces. From each piece keep back one-third for the lid. Roll out the pastry and use to line four 10 cm (4 inch) wide, 3 cm (1¼ inch) deep Yorkshire pudding tins. Roll out the lids.

Mix the sausage meat, mixed herbs and mustard together and season.

Cut the hard-boiled eggs in half and place a half in the bottom of each case, cut side down. Top with the sausage meat.

Brush the edges of the pies with the beaten egg, position the lids and press well together. Cut into the edges with a sharp knife to decorate. Make a small hole in the centre of each pie.

Using the pastry trimmings, make two or three leaves for each pie and a little pastry rose to go round each hole in the middle. Brush with beaten egg to glaze.

Cook for 30–35 minutes until the pastry is golden brown. Cool in the tins. When cool, lift the roses off the pies and fill each with cooling jelly, if using. Chill.

Tip A pinch of salt in the beaten egg makes a very glossy glaze.

Scotch eggs

Rumour has it that these were invented by Fortnum & Mason in 1738. They're traditionally served cold and are having something of a revival.

Makes 6
Preparation time:
  20 minutes
Cooking time:
  18–24 minutes

6 **eggs**
400 g (14 oz) **pork sausage meat**
2 tablespoons **plain flour**
salt and freshly ground **black pepper**
1 **egg**, beaten
8 tablespoons **breadcrumbs**
vegetable oil, for deep frying
watercress or **parsley**, to garnish

Add the eggs to a small pan of water, bring to the boil and simmer for 6 minutes. Rinse with cold water and peel while still hot. Cool in cold water.

Divide the sausage meat into six equal pieces and pat out into rounds.

Put some flour on a plate, season, dip each egg in the flour and cover with the sausage meat.

Flour again, dip in the beaten egg and roll in the breadcrumbs.

Heat the oil in a deep heavy-bottomed pan until it reaches 180°C/350°F on a sugar thermometer or until a breadcrumb sizzles and turns brown when dropped into the oil. Cook two eggs at a time for 6–8 minutes until golden brown. Wait for the oil to heat up again before cooking the next batch.

Carefully drain with a slotted spoon on to kitchen towel. Cut into halves and serve garnished with watercress or parsley.

Tips To cook in the oven, place on a baking tray and bake at 190°C/375°F/Gas Mark 5 for 25 minutes until golden brown.

To make these even more tasty, use skinned gourmet sausages instead of the sausage meat. Try garlicky Toulouse sausages, pork and apple, or pork, pancetta and Parmesan.

Quiche Lorraine

Quiche Lorraine became popular in Britain after World War II and features in most WI recipe books. This recipe is delicious served hot or cold.

Serves **6–8**
Preparation time:
30 minutes +
45–50 minutes
chilling
Cooking time:
65 minutes

6 rashers **streaky bacon**, rind removed
1 small **onion**, finely chopped
110 g (4 oz) mature **Cheddar cheese**, grated
2 **eggs**
150 ml (5 fl oz) **full-fat milk** or **single cream**
25 g (1 oz) **butter,** melted
salt and freshly ground **black pepper**
a little **cayenne pepper**

Pastry
80 g (3 oz) **butter**
175 g (6 oz) **plain flour**

To make the pastry, rub the butter into the flour until it resembles breadcrumbs. Add enough cold water to make the crumb mixture come together to form a firm dough, wrap in cling film and chill in the fridge for 30 minutes.

Roll out the pastry on a lightly floured surface and line a well-greased 22 cm (8½ inch) flan dish. Chill again for 15–20 minutes. Preheat the oven to 190°C/375°F/Gas Mark 5.

Remove the pastry from the fridge, line the base with baking parchment and then fill it with baking beans. Place on a baking tray and bake blind for 20 minutes. Remove the beans and parchment and return to the oven for another 5 minutes to dry and crisp the base. Remove from the oven and increase the temperature to 200°C/400°F/Gas Mark 6.

Meanwhile, fry the bacon lightly with the onion. Cut the rashers in half and cover the pastry with the bacon, onion and cheese.

Beat the eggs, cream and melted butter together and season with salt, pepper and a little cayenne pepper.

Pour over the bacon mixture and bake for 40 minutes until set and golden brown.

Harvest sausage rolls

These are a far cry from processed sausage rolls bought in a supermarket. The pastry can be lightened by using half plain and half wholemeal flour.

Makes 10–14,
  depending on size
Preparation time:
  20 minutes +
  30 minutes chilling
Cooking time:
  20–30 minutes

60 g (2 oz) **margarine**
60 g (2 oz) **white vegetable fat**
225 g (8 oz) **plain wholemeal flour**
a pinch of **salt**
1 **egg**, beaten
225 g (8 oz) **pork sausage meat**
½ teaspoon **dried sage**
25 g (1 oz) **bran**
Home-made mustard, to serve (see recipe)

Preheat the oven to 200°C/400°F/Gas Mark 6.

Make the pastry by rubbing both fats into the flour and salt in a large bowl. Add about 60 ml (2 fl oz) of cold water, or enough to bring the mixture together to form a dough. Wrap in cling film and chill for 30 minutes.

Roll out half the pastry to a 20 × 10 cm (11 × 4 inch) strip. Do the same with the other half. Leave the strips to relax while you prepare the filling.

Mix half the egg into the sausage meat with the sage. Wash and dry your hands and dust in wholemeal flour (or use latex gloves). Mould the sausage meat into two rolls the length of the pastry strips. Put one on each of the strips.

Brush a little beaten egg along one edge of each strip and fold over. Press the edges firmly together. Brush each roll with the remaining beaten egg and sprinkle with the bran. Cut diagonally to make individual sausage rolls. Put on a baking tray and bake for 20–30 minutes. Cool on a wire rack and eat hot or cold with mustard.

Home-made mustard
Home-made mustard makes these special sausage rolls even more delicious.

50 g (1¾ oz) each **black** and **white mustard seeds**
150 ml (5 fl oz) **herb vinegar**
3 tablespoons runny **honey**
1 teaspoon **salt**
½ teaspoon **mace**

Put all the ingredients into a bowl and leave overnight to soften the seeds.

Mix in a blender until thick and creamy. If too thick, add a little more vinegar. Leave a proportion of the seeds whole – do not blend until there are no seeds to be seen.

Store in small jars with plastic lids. Keep airtight or the mustard will dry out.

Vary the flavour with different spices, vinegars and more or less honey.

Anchovy eggs

An interesting Breconshire variation on traditional egg mayonnaise. The anchovy gives a piquant flavour to the eggs.

Serves 4
Preparation time:
25 minutes

4 hard-boiled **eggs**, peeled
a little **salt**
a little **cayenne pepper**
2 teaspoons **anchovy essence**
2 tablespoons **mayonnaise**
8 small slices **brown bread**
butter
2 **tomatoes**, each cut into 4 slices, discarding the ends
a little fresh **parsley**, to garnish

Halve the eggs and remove the yolks. Place the yolks in a bowl with a little salt and cayenne pepper, the anchovy essence and mayonnaise and mix it all together to create a moist paste.

Spoon the paste into a piping bag and pipe it back into the egg whites. Alternatively, spoon the mixture straight into the cavities.

Butter the bread and cut into small rounds. Place a thin round of tomato on each round and half an egg on top. Garnish with a little fresh parsley.

Pinwheel sandwiches

An attractive and practical way to serve sandwiches for a party. Each filling is sufficient for one large loaf.

Makes 80–120 pinwheels
Preparation time: 45 minutes + chilling

1 large **white** or **brown tin loaf**, uncut and chilled for ease of cutting
about 175 g (6 oz) **butter**, softened, or **low-fat spread**

Crab and gherkin filling
2–3 large jars **crab paste**
jar midget **gherkins**

Egg and cress filling
6 **eggs**
3–4 tablespoons **mayonnaise**
3 cartons **mustard and cress**, chopped
salt and freshly ground **black pepper**

Cut off the crust all round the loaf. Cut off a 1-cm (½-inch) thick slice from the long side, keeping it even. Repeat to get 10 slices. A good baker can do this for you. Butter each slice of bread.

For the crab and gherkin pinwheels, spread each slice with crab paste and then arrange a line of drained midget gherkins along one short edge. Roll up tightly, beginning at the edge with the gherkins, wrap at once in cling film and refrigerate until required. Slice each roll into 8–12 pinwheels.

For the egg and cress pinwheels, add the eggs to a small pan of water, bring to the boil and simmer for 6 minutes. Rinse with cold water and peel. Cool the hard-boiled eggs in cold water and then dry on kitchen towel. Mash finely, adding the mayonnaise, mustard and cress and seasoning. Spread each slice with this mixture, roll up, wrap in cling film and refrigerate until required. Slice each roll into 8–12 pinwheels.

Tip Make these the day before to make sure they hold together, then simply cut into slices when required.

Whitstable sandwiches

The coastal town of Whitstable in Kent is famed for its seafood. Spread this quick and tasty filling between slices of buttered bread or on pieces of toast.

Serves 4
Preparation time:
  15 minutes + 2 hours
  marinating

250 g (9 oz) cooked, peeled
  shrimp or **prawns**
2 **spring onions**, sliced
2 tablespoons **French**
  dressing
3 **eggs**
2 tablespoons finely
  chopped **lettuce**
2 tablespoons finely
  chopped **watercress**
Old-fashioned salad cream
  (see recipe)
8 slices **wholemeal bread**
butter, softened

Cover the shrimps or prawns and spring onions with the French dressing and leave to marinate for 2 hours.

Meanwhile, add the eggs to a small pan of water, bring to the boil and simmer for 6 minutes. Rinse with cold water and peel. Cool in cold water, dry on kitchen towel and halve.

Separate the egg yolks from the whites. Pass the yolks through a sieve to mash them and chop the whites finely. Mix into the shrimp or prawn mixture with the lettuce and watercress and a little salad cream.

Butter the bread and divide the mixture between four of the slices. Top with the remaining slices and cut into triangles.

Old-fashioned salad cream
This recipe from food writer Margaret Ryan featured in the WI magazine *Home & Country* in July 1969.

25 g (1 oz) **plain flour**
2 tablespoons **caster sugar**
1 teaspoon **salt**
½ teaspoon freshly ground **black pepper**
1 **egg**
1 tablespoon **English mustard powder**
1 tablespoon **sunflower** or **extra virgin olive oil**
600 ml (20 fl oz) **milk**
150 ml (5 fl oz) **white wine vinegar**

Sift the flour, sugar, salt and pepper into a bowl. Beat the egg in another bowl, add the mustard and the oil and beat again. Add the milk, stirring well all the time. Add the milk mixture gradually to the flour, making a thin paste and then stirring in the rest. If you have a blender, give it a whizz.

Pour into a small saucepan and place over a moderate heat. Cook, stirring all the time, until it boils. Continue to cook for 3–4 minutes, stirring constantly. When the mixture is very thick, smooth and creamy, take it off the heat and let it cool for a few moments before adding the vinegar and giving it a final whisk.

Cornish potato cake

This 'winter teatime savoury' is not quite as famous as the Cornish pasty, but it's a great way to use up your potatoes.

Serves 6–8
Preparation time:
   30 minutes
Cooking time:
   20–30 minutes

450 g (1 lb) peeled **potatoes**
   (weighed after peeling)
salt
110 g (4 oz) **plain flour**
60 g (2 oz) **butter**
white pepper

Boil the potatoes in lightly salted water until they are cooked. Strain and tip into a bowl. Preheat the oven to 220°C/425°F/Gas Mark 7.

Add the flour and butter to the hot potatoes and mash thoroughly together. Season with salt and white pepper.

Spoon on to a greased baking tray and press out with your hands to about 5 mm (¼ inch) thick. Score the top criss-cross wise with a fork and bake in the oven for 20–30 minutes until nicely browned.

Cut into pieces and serve at once.

Tip Alternatively, you could cut the potato cakes into circles using a saucer and bake individually on a tray.

Cakes
and special occasions

Victoria sandwich

Sweet, fluffy, and unmistakably British – the Victoria sandwich still reigns supreme at village fêtes and on afternoon tea menus across the nation.

Serves 6
Preparation time:
  20 minutes
Baking time:
  25–30 minutes

110 g (4 oz) soft **margarine**
110 g (4 oz) **caster sugar**,
  plus extra for decorating
2 **eggs**
110 g (4 oz) **self-raising flour**
raspberry jam, for filling

Preheat the oven to 180°C/350°F/Gas Mark 4. Grease two 15 cm (6 inch) sandwich tins and line with non-stick baking parchment or greased greaseproof paper.

Cream the margarine and sugar together until light and creamy in texture.

Add the eggs a little at a time and beat well. Sift the flour and gently fold into the mixture.

Divide the mixture between the two prepared tins and bake in the oven for 25–30 minutes until well risen and the tops spring back when lightly pressed with a fingertip.

When cold, fill with jam and sprinkle the top with caster sugar.

Variations This recipe is taken from the *Cumbria–Cumberland WI Cookery Book* and can be adapted to make 20 small sweet buns.

Queen cakes – add 40 g (1½ oz) of currants.

Coffee – add 1 teaspoon of coffee essence or coffee water.

Walnut – add 60 g (2 oz) of chopped walnuts.

Orange – add the grated zest of ½ an orange.

Chocolate fudge cake

A rich chocolatey cake based on a recipe from the *Northumberland WI Cookery Book*, 1969. The chocolate fudge icing is a delicious addition.

Makes 20 squares
Preparation time:
  20 minutes + cooling
Baking time:
  25–30 minutes

40 g (1½ oz) **cocoa powder**
5 tablespoons boiling **water**
175 g (6 oz) soft **margarine**
  or **butter**
175 g (6 oz) **caster sugar**
3 **eggs**
1 teaspoon **vanilla essence**
175 g (6 oz) **self-raising flour**
1½ teaspoons **baking
  powder**
crystallised rose petals,
  crushed, to decorate

Chocolate fudge icing
100 g (3½ oz) **plain
  chocolate** (70% cocoa
  solids), broken into pieces
60 g (2 oz) **butter**, diced
2 tablespoons **double cream**

Preheat the oven to 180°C/350°F/Gas Mark 4. Line an 18 x 28 cm (7 x 11 inch) roasting tin or cake tin with a large piece of non-stick baking parchment, snipping diagonally into the corners of the paper and pressing into the tin so that the base and sides are lined.

Place the cocoa powder in a small bowl, gradually mix in the boiling water until you get a smooth paste and set aside to cool.

Cream the margarine or butter and sugar together until light and fluffy. Gradually beat in the eggs and vanilla essence with a spoonful of the flour.

Mix the remaining flour with the baking powder and then stir into the mixture with the cooled cocoa paste until smooth.

Spoon into the prepared tin, spread into an even layer and bake for 25–30 minutes until well risen and the top springs back when lightly pressed with a fingertip.

Leave to cool for 10 minutes and then lift the cake from the tin using the paper. Peel down the paper on the sides and leave to cool on a wire rack

To make the icing, melt the chocolate in a bowl over a pan of simmering water. Add the butter and stir to melt. Add the cream and stir until smooth and glossy.

Spread the icing over the cake, sprinkle with crushed crystallised rose petals and leave to set. Cut into 20 pieces, lift off the base paper and transfer to a serving plate. Serve in cupcake cases, if liked.

Madeira cake

This buttery lemon sponge is delicious taken with tea or with a mid-morning glass of Madeira wine.

Serves 8
Preparation time:
   20 minutes + cooling
Baking time:
   35–40 minutes

110 g (4 oz) **butter**, softened
110 g (4 oz) **caster sugar**
a pinch of **salt**
3 **eggs**, lightly beaten
140 g (5 oz) **self-raising flour**
finely grated zest of 1 **lemon**

Preheat the oven to 180°C/350°F/Gas Mark 4. Grease a 15 cm (6 inch) round cake tin and line with non-stick baking parchment or greased greaseproof paper.

Beat the butter and sugar together with the salt until very light and creamy.

Add the eggs one at a time, beating each one in thoroughly. Lastly, fold in the flour and lemon zest.

Pour the cake mixture into the prepared tin and bake for 35–40 minutes until well risen and the top springs back when lightly pressed with a fingertip. Turn out on a wire rack to cool.

Tip This mixture can be used as a base for a fruit cake – just add 110 g (4 oz) of currants, 60 g (2 oz) of sultanas and a little mixed peel.

Saffron cake

Yellow saffron cake is as much a delicacy in Cornwall as the Cornish pasty. It is popularly believed that the Phoenicians first brought it to the country.

Serves 8
Preparation time:
  20 minutes + proving
  + cooling
Baking time:
  50 minutes

200 ml (7 fl oz) warm **milk** or half and half warm **milk** and **water**
25 g (1 oz) **fast action dried yeast**
175 g (6 oz) **caster sugar**
900 g (2 lb) **plain flour**
350 g (12 oz) **butter**
1 teaspoon **salt**
60 g (2 oz) **mixed peel**
450 g (1 lb) **currants**
1 teaspoon **saffron**

Place the warm milk or milk and water in a bowl and add the yeast, 1 teaspoon of the sugar and a couple of heaped spoonfuls of the flour. Stir, cover and set aside,

In a large bowl, rub the butter into the remaining flour until the mixture resembles breadcrumbs and then mix in the salt, peel, currants and remaining sugar.

Roll the saffron between two pieces of greaseproof paper to crumble it and then steep it in a little hot water. Add to the cake mixture with the yeast and liquid mixture to form a dough.

Knead well on an unfloured work surface for 8–10 minutes. Some of the currants will escape – simply put them back in the dough at the end of kneading. Cover with oiled cling film or a clean, damp tea towel and set aside until doubled in size (the time this takes will depend on the warmth of the room).

Knead again. Grease a 900 g (2 lb) loaf tin and put the dough in the tin to prove. Cover with oiled cling film or a clean, damp tea towel and set aside until doubled in size again. Preheat the oven to 190°C/375°F/Gas Mark 5.

Bake for 25 minutes and then reduce the temperature to 180°C/350°F/Gas Mark 4 and bake for a further 25 minutes. Cool in the tin for a few minutes before turning out on to a wire rack.

Fruity marmalade cake

The addition of marmalade to this fruit cake gives it a subtle spicy flavour. Don't worry if your fruit sinks a little – it will still taste great.

Serves 8
Preparation time:
30 minutes + cooling
Baking time: 1 hour
50 minutes–2 hours

225 g (8 oz) **self-raising flour**
¼ level teaspoon **mixed spice**
¼ level teaspoon grated **nutmeg**
¼ level teaspoon **cinnamon**
a pinch of **salt**
110 g (4 oz) **caster sugar**
60 g (2 oz) **glacé cherries**, chopped
225 g (8 oz) dried **mixed fruit**
1 heaped tablespoon thick **orange marmalade**
3 **eggs**
6 tablespoons **milk**
a few drops of **vanilla extract**
110 g (4 oz) **butter**, melted
15 g (½ oz) **walnuts**, chopped

Preheat the oven to 150°C/300°F/Gas Mark 2.

Grease an 18 cm (7 inch) round cake tin, line with non-stick baking parchment or greased greaseproof paper and tie a piece of brown paper around the outside of the tin so that it stands about 5 cm (2 inches) above the tin.

Sift the flour, spices, salt and sugar into a bowl, add the cherries, dried fruit and marmalade and stir well.

Break the eggs one at a time into a jug and stir into the mixture. Add the milk, vanilla extract and melted butter.

Mix thoroughly and then beat with a wooden spoon for 3 minutes. Turn the mixture into the prepared tin.

Sprinkle the top of the mixture with the chopped walnuts and bake in the centre of the oven for 1 hour 50 minutes–2 hours. Check that the cake is cooked by inserting a skewer into the centre of the cake. If it comes out clean, the cake is ready.

Leave to cool in the tin for 30 minutes and then turn out on to a wire rack.

Carrot cake

This cake was revived in World War II as carrots were a cheap and healthy alternative to sugar and sweetened products.

Serves 8–12
Preparation time:
  30 minutes + cooling
Baking time: 40–45
  minutes

175 g (6 oz) soft **margarine**
110 g (4 oz) **light muscovado**
  sugar
2 **eggs**
250 g (9 oz) **self-raising flour**
½ teaspoon **ground**
  cinnamon
25 g (1 oz) **mixed peel** or
  marmalade
finely grated zest of
  1 **orange**
60 g (2 oz) **raisins**, washed
225 g (8 oz) finely grated
  carrots
4–5 tablespoons **milk** or
  orange juice

Cream cheese frosting
170 g (6 oz) **cream cheese**
60 g (2 oz) soft **margarine** or
  butter
110 g (4 oz) **icing sugar**
a few drops **vanilla extract**

Preheat the oven to 180°C/350°F/Gas Mark 4. Lightly grease an 18 cm (7 inch) square or a 20 cm (8 inch) round cake tin.

Cream the margarine with the sugar until light and creamy. Whisk the eggs and beat into the mixture.

Sieve the flour with the cinnamon and fold into the creamed mixture together with the peel or marmalade, orange zest and raisins.

Mix in the grated carrots. Add sufficient milk or orange juice to give a dropping consistency. Pour the mixture into the prepared tin and smooth over the top.

Bake for 40–45 minutes until golden brown, firm to the touch and a skewer comes out clean when inserted into the centre of the cake. Cool in the tin for 15 minutes and then turn out on to a wire rack.

For the frosting, cream together the cream cheese and margarine or butter and then beat in the icing sugar and vanilla extract. Use to cover the top of the cake and then cut into 8–12 servings.

Tip Decorate with bought sugar carrot decorations or make your own with ready -to-roll orange and green fondant icing.

Génoise sponge cake

A Génoise cake is a whisked sponge enriched with melted butter. It is the perfect base for gâteaux and petits fours.

Serves 6–8
Preparation time:
  30 minutes + cooling
Baking time:
  20–30 minutes

4 eggs
125 g (4½ oz) **caster sugar**
100 g (3½ oz) **fine plain flour**
100 g (3½ oz) **butter**

Preheat the oven to 180°C/350°F/Gas Mark 4. Lightly oil a 20 cm (8 inch) cake tin and line it carefully with non-stick baking parchment or greased greaseproof paper.

Break the eggs into a large bowl, add the sugar and whisk over a pan of simmering water until the mixture has almost doubled in bulk and the whisk leaves a heavy trail. Take off the heat and continue to whisk for a minute or two.

Sift the flour twice to incorporate as much air as possible. Melt the butter in a small pan and cool until just runny. Fold the flour into the mixture with the melted butter. Mix swiftly but gently.

Turn into the prepared tin and cook for 20–30 minutes until the cake is just shrinking from the sides of the tin. Turn out on to a cloth, invert on to a wire rack and leave to cool.

Tip This is delicious filled with cream and jam and/or fruit.

Cherry cake

If you wash the cherries in warm water and dry thoroughly, this takes away the stickiness that is apt to make them sink to the bottom of the cake.

Serves 8
Preparation time:
25 minutes + cooling
Baking time: 1 hour
30 minutes

175 g (6 oz) **butter**, softened
175 g (6 oz) **caster sugar**,
plus 1 level tablespoon
for decoration
3 **eggs**, beaten
250 g (9 oz) **plain flour**
2½ level teaspoons **baking**
powder
1 tablespoon **milk**
350 g (12 oz) **glacé cherries**,
quartered but leaving 3
whole

Preheat the oven to 190°C/375°F/Gas Mark 5. Grease a 15 cm (6 inch) square cake tin and line with non-stick baking parchment or greased greaseproof paper.

Beat the butter to a soft cream and then beat in the caster sugar. Add the eggs to the mixture, a little at a time.

Sieve the flour and baking powder together and stir lightly into the mixture with the milk. Add the quartered cherries and stir them evenly through the mixture.

Turn into the prepared tin. Smooth the top and make a slight hollow in the centre. Sprinkle the tablespoon of sugar on top. Cut the three remaining cherries in half and dot them over the top.

Bake in the centre of the oven for 20 minutes, then reduce the temperature to 180°C/350°F/Gas Mark 4 and bake for a further 40 minutes. Lastly, reduce the temperature again to 150°C/300°F/Gas Mark 2 and bake for 30 minutes.

Leave to cool in the tin for 10 minutes and then turn out on to a wire rack.

Coffee cake

Bringing an air of sophistication to afternoon tea, no teatime gathering is complete without a slice of coffee cake.

Serves 8
Preparation time:
30 minutes + cooling
Baking time:
20–25 minutes

175 g (6 oz) **butter**, softened
175 g (6 oz) **light brown soft sugar**
1 tablespoon strong **coffee** (see Tip) or a few drops of **coffee essence**
3 **eggs**, lightly beaten
175 g (6 oz) **self-raising flour**
1 teaspoon **baking powder**

Butter cream
110 g (4 oz) **butter**, softened
225 g (8 oz) **icing sugar**
2 tablespoons strong **coffee** (see Tip) or 1 teaspoon **coffee essence**
80 g (3 oz) **walnuts**, chopped

To decorate
icing sugar
8 walnut halves

Preheat the oven to 180°C/350°F/Gas Mark 4. Grease two 20 cm (8 inch) sandwich tins and base line with non-stick baking parchment or greased greaseproof paper.

Cream the butter and sugar together, add the coffee and beat in the eggs little by little, keeping the mixture stiff. Sift the flour and baking powder together and fold in.

Divide the mixture between the prepared tins and bake for 20–25 minutes until risen and the tops spring back when lightly pressed with a fingertip.

Allow to cool in the tins for a few minutes then turn out, peel away the paper and cool on a wire rack.

Make the butter cream by blending the butter, icing sugar and coffee together until smooth.

Take one cake and arrange wooden skewers over the top to mark out eight portions. Sieve icing sugar over the top and then remove the skewers. Pipe on eight butter cream rosettes and top each with a walnut piece.

Add the chopped walnuts to the remaining butter cream and spread over the second cake. Put the first cake on top of this.

Tip Strong coffee for the cake and butter cream can be made from 2 teaspoons of instant coffee dissolved in 3 tablespoons of boiling water.

Party rings

Light rings of choux pastry filled with fresh fruit and cream complete any tea table. You could also fill these with nectarines or strawberries.

Makes 6
Preparation time:
  35 minutes
Baking time:
  20–25 minutes

2 ripe **peaches**
boiling water
275 ml (10 fl oz) **whipping** or
  double cream, whipped
150 g (5½ oz) **raspberries**
100 g (3½ oz) **icing sugar**

Choux pastry
60 g (2 oz) **butter**, diced
70 g (2½ oz) **strong white
  flour**
1 teaspoon **caster sugar**
2 **eggs**, beaten

Preheat the oven to 200°C/400°F/Gas Mark 6. Put the oven shelf in the top half of the oven if your oven isn't fan assisted. Grease a baking tray.

To make the choux pastry, put 150 ml (5 fl oz) of cold water and the butter in a saucepan. Place over a medium heat until the butter has melted and it all comes to the boil. Meanwhile, sieve the flour on to a sheet of baking parchment that has been folded in half.

Remove the butter water from the heat and 'shoot' the flour into the mixture with the sugar. Beat vigorously with a wooden spoon (or use an electric hand whisk) until you have a smooth ball of paste.

Add the eggs gradually, beating well between each addition until the paste is smooth and glossy. Spoon the mixture into a piping bag with a 1 cm (½ inch) plain nozzle. Sprinkle water on to the baking tray and tap to get rid of any excess.

Pipe the pastry into six 7.5 cm (3 inch) circles. Bake for 15–20 minutes until well risen and golden brown.

Make a small slit in each ring to let the steam escape and return to the oven for a couple of minutes to dry out the centres. Set aside on a wire rack to cool.

Dip the peaches in boiling water. Skin them and cut them into small pieces. Split the rings in half and fill the bottom half of the pastry ring with the whipped cream. Top with the peaches and raspberries and replace the lid.

Mix the icing sugar with 3–4 teaspoons of water to make a glacé icing. Drizzle the icing over the rings to decorate.

Tip The pastry rings can be made in the morning or the day before. Put them into an absolutely airtight tin when cold. They can then be filled just before the party.

Chocolate walnut cake

Chocolate is an unusual addition in this lightly spiced fruit cake but works extremely well – an absolute delight.

Serves 8–12
Preparation time:
 25 minutes + cooling
Baking time: 1½ hours

350 g (12 oz) **self-raising flour**
½ teaspoon **ground cinnamon**
½ teaspoon **mixed spice**
175 g (6 oz) soft **margarine**
60 g (2 oz) **walnuts**, roughly chopped
60 g (2 oz) **plain chocolate** (70% cocoa solids), roughly chopped
175 g (6 oz) **raisins**
175 g (6 oz) **demerara sugar**, plus 1 tablespoon for the topping
2 **eggs**, beaten
about 150 ml (5 fl oz) **milk**

Preheat the oven to 180°C/350°F/Gas Mark 4. Lightly grease a 20 cm (8 inch) round or an 18 cm (7 inch) square cake tin and line with non-stick baking parchment or greased greaseproof paper.

Sieve the flour and spices into a mixing bowl and rub in the margarine. Stir the walnuts, chocolate and raisins into the mixture, together with the sugar.

Stir the eggs into the dry ingredients, together with three-quarters of the milk. Mix thoroughly, adding enough of the remaining milk to give a soft dropping consistency.

Place in the prepared tin, smooth over the top and sprinkle with the sugar for the topping.

Bake for 1 hour and then reduce the oven temperature to 150°C/300°F/Gas Mark 2. Bake for a further 30 minutes until the cake is firm to the touch and a skewer inserted in the centre comes out clean.

Cool the cake in the tin for 10–15 minutes and then turn out on to a wire rack.

Meringue-topped cake

An unusual cake to delight your guests, the cherries and almonds add an extra delicious touch.

Serves 8
Preparation time:
  20 minutes
Baking time:
  25–30 minutes

175 g (6 oz) **self-raising flour**
¼ teaspoon **baking powder**
80 g (3 oz) soft **margarine** or **butter**
60 g (2 oz) **light brown soft sugar**
2 **eggs**, separated
110 g (4 oz) **icing sugar,** sieved
60 g (2 oz) **glacé cherries**, halved
25 g (1 oz) **flaked almonds**

Preheat the oven to 190°C/375°F/Gas Mark 5. Lightly grease a 25 x 18 cm (10 x 7 inch) or 20 cm (8 inch) round cake tin and line with non-stick baking parchment or greased greaseproof paper.

Sieve the flour and baking powder into a bowl, rub in the margarine or butter and mix in the sugar and egg yolks. Pour the mixture into the prepared tin.

Whisk the egg whites in a clean bowl until stiff peaks form. Fold in the icing sugar.

Spread the meringue mixture on top of the cake mixture and decorate with the cherries and flaked almonds.

Bake fairly near the top of the oven for 25–30 minutes, moving down to a middle shelf for the last 5 minutes. You may need to cover the top loosely with foil if the meringue browns too quickly.

Note This recipe is taken from the *Derbyshire WI Recipe Book*, a collection of recipes welcomed as a further contribution towards the development of the 'basis of all good housekeeping', reads the foreword. 'The countrywoman's reputation as a "good cook" is proverbial and the recipes contained in this book reflect the art and experience which has rightly and justly earned this reputation.'

Golden layer cake

Celebrate a special occasion with this regal cake from an old Yorkshire recipe. Don't be put off by all the stages – this is outstandingly good!

Serves 6–8
Preparation and baking
  time: 1 hour
  25–30 minutes

110 g (4 oz) **butter** or
  margarine, softened
110 g (4 oz) **light brown soft**
  sugar
225 g (8 oz) **plain flour**
1 level teaspoon **baking**
  powder
½ teaspoon **ground**
  cinnamon
½ teaspoon **ground nutmeg**
2 whole **eggs** and 1 **egg yolk**
150 ml (5 fl oz) **golden syrup**
70 ml (3 fl oz) **milk**

To decorate
1 tablespoon **golden syrup**
225 g (8 oz) **icing sugar**
3 dessertspoons **apricot jam**
25 g (1 oz) **walnuts**, chopped
175 g (6 oz) **light brown soft**
  sugar
1 **egg** white
1 teaspoon **vanilla extract**
walnut halves

Preheat the oven to 180°C/350°F/ Gas Mark 4. Grease two 20 cm (8 inch) deep loose-bottomed sandwich tins.

Beat the butter or margarine and sugar together until soft and creamy.

Sift the flour with the baking powder and spices. Whisk the whole eggs and egg yolk together. Heat the golden syrup slightly by warming it in the microwave for 20 seconds and add to the whisked eggs. Whisk together.

Gradually add the flour and egg mixtures into the creamed fat and sugar, alternating them, mixing well and adding the milk to moisten.

Divide the mixture between the two prepared tins, spread evenly and bake for 25–30 minutes, turning the cakes during cooking to make sure they rise evenly. Leave to rest for a few moments before turning out of the tins and setting aside to cool.

For the first filling, warm the golden syrup and mix with 1 dessertspoon of hot water. Add this to the icing sugar with enough extra hot water to make a thick coating consistency.

For the second filling, mix the jam and chopped walnuts together. If the jam is very stiff, it may need to be warmed slightly.

Halve each cake and cover one half of each with the syrup and sugar filling, pouring it into the centre and spreading it to the edge. Sandwich together again. Now sandwich the two whole cakes together with a thick layer of the jam and walnut filling.

To make the icing, put the brown sugar in a large mixing bowl with 35 ml (1 fl oz) of cold water and add the egg white and vanilla extract. Whisk together over hot water, preferably using an electric hand whisk, until the mixture becomes stiff. Spread a thin layer over the top and sides of the cake to stick the crumbs in place and then spoon over generously and spread into swirls with a round bladed knife. Leave until set and decorate with the walnut halves.

Tip Test a little of the icing on a plate to see if it will set before spreading it on the cake. If it is not ready, whisk for a little longer.

Festival tartlets

Dark chocolate cases filled with moist raspberry sponge – utterly decadent.
You could cheat by buying the chocolate cases.

Makes 8
Preparation time:
  30 minutes + 2 hours
  chilling

110 g (4 oz) **plain chocolate**
  (70% cocoa solids),
  broken into pieces
110 g (4 oz) **sponge cake**,
  crumbled
2 tablespoons **raspberry**
  jam
1 tablespoon **Kirsch** or
  brandy
125 ml (4 fl oz) **whipping**
  cream, whipped
8 **raspberries** or **cherries**
angelica, cut into leaf
  shapes (optional)

Place the chocolate in a bowl over a pan of simmering water and stir until melted. Brush eight cupcake paper cases (use two together if flimsy) with the melted chocolate, making sure it is in an even layer. Leave to set for 10 minutes and then brush the insides of the cases again with chocolate, re-melting if necessary and again making sure it is in an even layer. Chill for a couple of hours.

Mix the crumbled sponge cake with the jam and Kirsch to give a soft consistency.

Carefully peel the paper cases away from the chocolate and divide the cake mixture between the chocolate cases.

Decorate with the whipped cream, raspberries or cherries and angelica leaves, if using.

Tip Put the chocolate-coated paper cases in a bun tin to set. This will help them set to a nice round shape.

Birthday cake

This is a special occasion fruit cake, perfect for an afternoon tea party. Don't be put off by the long ingredients list – it really is very simple.

Serves 12
Preparation time:
  25 minutes + cooling
Baking time:
  4–4½ hours

250 g (9 oz) **plain flour**
¼ teaspoon **salt**
2 teaspoons **baking powder**
1 teaspoon **mixed spice**
½ teaspoon **ground cinnamon**
½ teaspoon **ground nutmeg**
225 g (8 oz) **currants**
225 g (8 oz) **sultanas**
225 g (8 oz) **raisins**
110 g (4 oz) **glacé cherries**
225 g (8 oz) soft **margarine**
225 g (8 oz) **light brown soft sugar**
5 **eggs**
1 tablespoon **black treacle**
110 g (4 oz) **mixed peel**
grated zest of 1 **lemon**
grated zest of 1 **orange**
1 tablespoon **lemon juice**
2 tablespoons **sherry**
60 g (2 oz) **ground almonds**
60 g (2 oz) **blanched almonds**, chopped

Preheat the oven to 150°C/300°F/Gas Mark 2. Grease a 20 cm (8 inch) square or a 23 cm (9 inch) round cake tin and line with doubled non-stick baking parchment or greased greaseproof paper. Place a double thickness of brown paper around the outside of the tin to protect the sides of the cake during cooking.

Sieve the flour with the salt, baking powder and spices. Wash the dried fruit and quarter and wash the glacé cherries. Dry thoroughly.

Place all the ingredients in a mixing bowl and beat together until well blended. Place in the prepared tin and hollow out the centre a little.

Bake for 1 hour and then reduce the oven temperature to 140°C/275°F/Gas Mark 1 and continue to cook for a further 3–3½ hours or until the cake is firm to the touch and beginning to shrink slightly from the sides of the tin. It may be necessary to place a sheet of foil or greaseproof paper over the cake to prevent it over-browning.

Leave in the tin until cold and then turn out. Wrap in greaseproof paper and foil, store to mature the cake, then ice or use as desired.

Lemon cake

There are many WI variations on the classic lemon cake, or lemon drizzle cake as it is commonly known.

Serves 8
Preparation time:
 20 minutes + cooling
Baking time:
 50–60 minutes

175 g (6 oz) soft **margarine**
175 g (6 oz) **caster sugar**
2 **eggs**, lightly beaten
4 tablespoons **milk**
175 g (6 oz) **self-raising flour**, sieved
finely grated zest and juice of 1 large **lemon**
1 tablespoon **icing sugar**

Preheat the oven to 180°C/350°F/Gas Mark 4. Lightly grease a 900 g (2 lb) loaf tin and line with non-stick baking parchment or greased greaseproof paper.

Cream the margarine and caster sugar together until light and creamy and then gradually beat in the eggs together with the milk.

Lightly fold in the sieved flour and lemon zest. Place in the prepared tin and smooth the top.

Bake for 50–60 minutes or until the cake is golden brown, firm to the touch and beginning to shrink from the sides of the tin.

Mix the lemon juice with the icing sugar and pour over the cake as soon as it has been taken out of the oven.

Allow the glaze to set, remove the cake from the tin and place on a wire rack to cool.

Note The Lancashire WI's 'Luscious Lemon Cake' (taken from the *Lancashire Cook Book*'s Diamond Jubilee edition) advises pricking the cake all over with a fork while still warm. The icing then seeps into the cake to ensure it's really moist.

Strawberry jelly cake

Quintessentially British, strawberries and cream make the perfect addition to afternoon tea. Layer with buttery crumbs for a decadent dessert.

Serves 6
Preparation time:
1 hour + chilling
Cooking time:
10–15 minutes

110 g (4 oz) **butter**, softened
60 g (2 oz) **demerara sugar**
60 g (2 oz) **walnuts**, finely
   chopped
110 g (4 oz) **plain flour**
2 x 12 g sachets powdered
   gelatine
450 g (1 lb) **strawberries**,
   hulled and thickly sliced
1 teaspoon **lemon juice**
175 g (6 oz) **caster sugar**
300 ml (10 fl oz) **double**
   cream

Preheat the oven to 200°C/400°F/Gas Mark 6. Rub the butter, demerara sugar, walnuts and flour together. Scatter this mixture over a shallow tin and bake for 10–15 minutes. Leave to cool and then crumble into a mixing bowl.

Place the gelatine in a small bowl with 4 tablespoons of water and leave to soften for a few minutes.

Mash a quarter of the strawberries in a small saucepan and add the lemon juice and caster sugar. Bring this mixture to the boil, take off the heat, add the softened gelatine and stir until completely dissolved.

Put a little of this mixture through a strainer into the base of a 1.2 litre (2 pint) jelly mould and chill for 15–20 minutes to set.

Whip the cream until it just holds its shape and then fold in the remaining sliced strawberries.

When the remaining gelatine mixture is cold and on the point of setting, fold it into the strawberries and cream. Immediately fill the mould with layers of the strawberry mixture and crumbs, starting with strawberry and ending with crumbs, gently pressing the crumbs into the cream mixture after each addition. Chill for 2–3 hours to set.

To serve, turn out of the mould. Dip the mould briefly in hot (but not boiling) water, loosen the edge of the cake with a fingertip, cover the mould with a plate, turn upside down and then jerk the plate and mould to release the jelly.

Tip If you like, decorate up to 1 hour before needed. Whip 150 ml (5 fl oz) of whipping or double cream, just until it holds its shape, then pipe it around the base of the cake. Arrange a large sliced strawberry around the cream.

Gâteau St Georges

This is a glamorous chocolate variation of lemon meringue pie – utterly irresistible.

Serves 8
Preparation time:
  40 minutes + cooling
Baking time:
  40–50 minutes

Génoise sponge cake mixture (see page 42)
110 g (4 oz) **dark chocolate** (70% cocoa solids), broken into pieces
3 **eggs**, separated
60 g (2 oz) **butter**, softened
2 teaspoons **rum**
110 g (4 oz) **caster sugar**
cocoa powder, to decorate

Preheat the oven to 180°C/350°F/Gas Mark 4. Grease a 20–23 cm (8–9 inch) sponge flan tin, base line with a round of non-stick baking parchment and grease again.

Pour the Génoise cake mixture into the tin and bake for 20–30 minutes until the cake starts to shrink away from the sides of the tin. Turn out and leave to cool.

Place the chocolate and 1 tablespoon of water in a bowl and melt over a pan of simmering water. When completely melted, remove from the heat.

Beat the egg yolks, one at a time, into the chocolate with the butter and the rum. When the butter is completely absorbed, pour the mixture on to the sponge. Leave to set. Preheat the oven to 160°C/325°F/Gas Mark 3.

Whisk the egg whites in a large clean bowl until stiff peaks form. Add the caster sugar a teaspoon at a time, whisking until all the sugar has been absorbed and you have a glossy meringue.

Swirl the meringue on to the set chocolate and cook until set on the outside, about 20 minutes. It need not dry out, but must be firmly set on top. Serve cold, decorated with a sprinkling of cocoa powder.

Tips A wooden spoon is too thick for any folding operation. The thin edge of a metal spoon cuts through mixtures without breaking down the airy texture.

To save time, or if you don't have a sponge flan tin, make this with a ready-bought sponge flan ring.

Instead of adding the rum to the chocolate mixture, try drizzling up to 2 tablespoons over the sponge flan.

Traditional
and regional
favourites

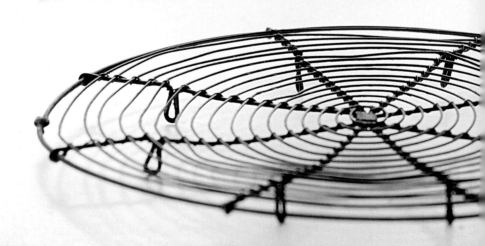

Eccles cakes

Named after the English town of Eccles, these delicious flat pastries also go by the name of squashed fly cakes due to their packed filling of currants.

Makes 10
Preparation time:
   40 minutes + 1 hour
   chilling + cooling
Cooking time:
   15 minutes

175 g (6 oz) **butter**
225 g (8 oz) **plain flour**
a pinch of **salt**
1 **egg white**
caster sugar, for sprinkling

Filling
60 g (2 oz) **demerara sugar**
60 g (2 oz) **butter**, softened
110 g (4 oz) **currants**
60 g (2 oz) **mixed peel**, finely
   chopped
¼ teaspoon **mixed spice**

To make the pastry, wrap the butter in foil and place it in the freezer for 30 minutes.

Sift the flour and salt into a bowl. Holding the butter with the foil, dip it into the flour and then grate it into the bowl using a coarse grater placed over the flour. Keep dipping the butter into the flour to make it easier to grate.

Using a palette knife, start to cut the butter into the flour until the mixture is crumbly. Add enough cold water (4–4½ tablespoons) to form a dough that leaves the bowl clean, place it in a polythene bag and chill for 30 minutes.

Meanwhile, for the filling, mix the sugar, butter, currants, peel and spice together in a bowl. Preheat the oven to 220°C/425°F/Gas Mark 7.

Roll out the pastry on a lightly floured surface to 4 mm (¼ inch) thick. Cut out 10 rounds using a 10 cm (4 inch) cutter, re-rolling the trimmings as necessary.

Place a teaspoonful of the mixture in the centre of each round pastry, wet the edges with water and pull them together to seal in the middle. Turn each round over and flatten with the rolling pin until the fruit is just visible or the rounds are about 7.5 cm (3 inches) in diameter. Make three cuts in the centre of each round.

Place on a greased baking tray, brush with the egg white and sprinkle with caster sugar. Bake for about 15 minutes until golden. Cool on a wire rack.

Old-fashioned treacle tart

For those with a sweet tooth, there can be few afternoon tea pastries to rival the treacle tart. Fruit rind and spice add a touch of luxury.

Serves 6
Preparation time:
 20 minutes +
 30 minutes chilling
Baking time:
 25–30 minutes

25 g (1 oz) **butter**
25 g (1 oz) **white vegetable fat**
110 g (4 oz) **plain flour**
a pinch of **salt**
clotted cream, to serve

Filling
8 tablespoons **golden syrup**
2 tablespoons **black treacle**
50 g (1¾ oz) **raisins**
25 g (1 oz) **mixed peel**
25 g (1 oz) **walnuts**, roughly chopped
finely grated zest of ½ **lemon**
finely grated zest of ½ **orange**
a good pinch of ground **allspice**
50 g (1¾ oz) fresh **breadcrumbs**

Preheat the oven to 200°C/400°F/Gas Mark 6.

Make the pastry by rubbing the butter and vegetable fat into the flour until the mixture resembles breadcrumbs. Add the salt and enough cold water to create a dough (4–5 teaspoons). Wrap in cling film and chill for 30 minutes.

Roll the pastry out fairly thinly on a lightly floured surface and use to line a 20 cm (8 inch) deep pie plate or flan dish. Prick the bottom of the pastry case with a fork, line with non-stick baking parchment or greaseproof paper, fill with baking beans and bake blind for 10 minutes. Remove the beans and paper and bake for a further 5 minutes to dry and crisp the base. Reduce the oven temperature to 180°C/350°F/Gas Mark 4.

Gently warm the syrup and treacle together.

Scatter the raisins, peel and walnuts into the pastry case and sprinkle with the fruit zest and allspice, reserving a little zest for decoration. Pour over the warmed syrup and treacle and sprinkle with the breadcrumbs, leaving for a few minutes to settle and soak in.

Bake for 25–30 minutes or until the filling is firm and the pastry lightly browned. Serve warm or cold with spoonfuls of clotted cream and decorated with the reserved fruit zest.

Battenburg cake

This chequered sponge is said to have first been baked to celebrate Prince Louis of Battenburg's marriage to Princess Victoria in 1884.

Serves 6
Preparation time:
20 minutes +
1–2 hours setting +
cooling
Baking time:
25–30 minutes

225 g (8 oz) **butter** or
  margarine, softened
225 g (8 oz) **caster sugar**
4 **eggs**
225 g (8 oz) **self-raising flour**
½ teaspoon **baking powder**
red **food colouring**
raspberry or **apricot jam**
225 g (8 oz) **marzipan**
icing sugar, for dusting

Preheat the oven to 180°C/350°F/Gas Mark 4. Grease two 900 g (2 lb) loaf tins and base line with non-stick baking parchment or greased greaseproof paper.

Cream the butter or margarine and sugar together and beat in the eggs. Sieve the flour and baking powder together, fold into the mixture and mix to a dropping consistency, adding a little hot water if necessary.

Put half the mixture into one of the prepared tins. Add a couple of drops of red food colouring to the remaining mixture to make it pale pink and put it into the second tin.

Bake for 25–30 minutes until a skewer inserted in the centre comes out clean. Allow to cool in the tin for a few minutes and then turn out on to a wire rack.

When cold, trim the cakes and cut two lengths from each one, each approximately 3 cm (1½ inches) square. Spread the pieces with jam and stick the four lengths together, the colours alternating. Wrap in greaseproof paper very tightly and leave for an hour or two.

Spread the outside of the cake with jam. Roll out the marzipan in a little icing sugar to an oblong the same width as the cake and long enough to wrap around.

Place the cake on the marzipan and wrap it around the cake, pressing it neatly and arranging the join in one lower corner. If you wish, crimp the edge and mark the top with a criss-cross pattern. Wrap the cake in paper again and keep for 3–4 hours in a cool place before eating.

Scones

Jam then cream? Or cream then jam? The age-old debate goes back and forth as scones continue to take centre stage at any good afternoon tea.

Makes 8–10
Preparation time:
  10 minutes + cooling
Baking time:
  12–15 minutes

225 g (8 oz) **plain flour**
¼ teaspoon **salt**
1 teaspoon **cream of tartar**
½ teaspoon **bicarbonate**
  of soda
60 g (2 oz) **butter**, diced
150 ml (5 fl oz) **milk** or
  buttermilk
1 **egg**, beaten, or **milk**,
  to glaze

Preheat the oven to 230°C/450°F/Gas Mark 8. Either grease a baking tray or dredge it liberally with flour.

Sift the flour, salt, cream of tartar and bicarbonate of soda into a bowl. Add the butter and rub in until the mixture resembles fine breadcrumbs.

Add enough milk or buttermilk to mix to a fairly soft dough using a palette knife or spatula.

Turn out on to a lightly floured surface and gently flatten the dough out to 2–2.5 cm (¾–1 inch) thick. Using a well-floured 4–5 cm (1½–2 inch) plain or fluted cutter, or an upturned glass, stamp out the scones.

Re-roll the trimmings to cut out more scones and place on the baking tray. Either brush the tops with the beaten egg or milk, or dredge lightly with flour.

Bake for 12–15 minutes until well risen, golden brown and just firm. Remove to a wire rack and leave to cool.

Tip Whatever your topping preference, these are best served warm on the day they are made – the perfect bridge between piles of sandwiches and cake. However, they reheat well and freeze for up to 3 months.

Variations **Fruit** – add 50 g (1¾ oz) of currants, sultanas, raisins or cut mixed peel to the dry ingredients.

Cheese – add a pinch of dried mustard and 40–50 g (1½–1¾ oz) of finely grated mature Cheddar cheese or 1–2 level tablespoons of grated Parmesan cheese to the dry ingredients.

Golden flapjacks

This delicious recipe, with a hint of coconut, hails from Worcestershire – sure proof that everyone has their own secret flapjack recipe.

Serves 6–8
Preparation time:
  20 minutes + cooling
Baking time:
  20 minutes

140 g (5 oz) **butter**
140 g (5 oz) **demerara sugar**
140 g (5 oz) **rolled oats**
3 drops **vanilla extract**
2 tablespoons **desiccated coconut**

Preheat the oven to 190°C/375°F/Gas Mark 5. Lightly grease a 30 × 20 cm (12 × 8 inch) Swiss roll tin.

Melt the butter over a low heat in a saucepan. Add the sugar, oats and vanilla extract. Mix well, add the coconut and mix again.

Turn out into the prepared tin and spread out with a fork, pressing down firmly.

Bake for 20 minutes or until golden brown. Cut into fingers while in the tin and leave to cool and crisp.

Note This recipe is from *The WI Recipe Book*, 1965 – a compilation of the best regional recipes sent in by WI members and described in the foreword as a 'unique collection of ways with food'.

Hot cross buns

A sticky hot cross bun is the ultimate Easter treat but can be enjoyed all year round. Eat them plain, toasted or spread with jam.

Makes 24
Preparation time:
  20 minutes + 2 hours rising + cooling
Baking time:
  15 minutes

900 g (2 lb) **strong white bread flour**
1 teaspoon **salt**
1–2 teaspoons **mixed spice**
4 teaspoons **fast action dried yeast**
110 g (4 oz) **caster sugar**, plus 2 level tablespoons for the glaze
110 g (4 oz) **butter**, diced
110 g (4 oz) **sultanas**
about 425 ml (15 fl oz) half and half warm **milk** and **water**
110 g (4 oz) **plain flour**

Place the bread flour, salt, mixed spice, yeast and sugar in a large bowl and mix together. Rub in the butter until the mixture resembles breadcrumbs and then add the sultanas.

Add the milk and water and mix to form a soft dough. Knead on a lightly floured surface for about 10 minutes until the dough is smooth and elastic.

Place in a clean, lightly oiled bowl, cover with oiled cling film or a clean tea towel and set aside in a warm place to rise for about 1½ hours or until doubled in size. Knead again for 2–3 minutes.

Divide the dough into 24 pieces, knead each piece until smooth and shape into buns. Place on lightly greased baking trays, allowing room for the buns to rise.

Cover with oiled cling film and leave in a warm place until doubled in size – about 30 minutes. Preheat the oven to 220°C/425°F/Gas Mark 7.

Mix the plain flour to a smooth paste with 8 tablespoons of water and spoon into a piping bag fitted with an 8 mm (⅜ inch) plain nozzle. Pipe crosses over the tops of the buns. Bake for 15 minutes or until brown and cooked.

While the buns are cooking, dissolve the 2 level tablespoons of sugar in 2 tablespoons of water. Bring to the boil and brush over the buns while still hot. Cool on a wire rack.

Pikelets

A warm pikelet (or crumpet) oozing with butter is the epitome of afternoon tea. Add jam with the butter or serve with syrup.

Makes 24–28
Preparation time:
  10 minutes +
  1½ hours rising
Cooking time:
  30 minutes

450 g (1 lb) **strong white bread flour**
¼ teaspoon **bicarbonate of soda**
1 teaspoon **caster sugar**
½ teaspoon **salt**
1½ teaspoons **fast action dried yeast**
600 ml (20 fl oz) half and half warm **milk** and **water**
butter, for greasing

Stir the flour, bicarbonate of soda, sugar, salt and yeast together in a large mixing bowl.

Gradually add the milk and water to make a smooth batter. Beat for a couple of minutes with a balloon whisk.

Cover with oiled cling film or a clean, damp tea towel, and leave to rise for up to 1½ hours in a warm place until the mixture is light and frothy.

Beat the batter again for about 1 minute.

Grease a griddle pan or heavy-based frying pan and heat. Drop tablespoons of the batter on to the griddle and cook for a couple of minutes. When the tops are covered in holes, turn over. Continue to cook for another 30 seconds; the pikelets should be golden brown one side and pale brown the other.

Continue to cook until all the batter has been used up. Serve straight away or cool on a wire rack.

Tip If you have them, use lightly greased 7.5 cm (3 inch) baking rings on the pan to create a nice neat shape for the pikelet. You can also create your own baking rings from lightly greased, washed tin cans with the labels, tops and bottoms removed.

Note This recipe is taken from the *National Federation of Women's Institutes' Yeast Cookery Book*, 1952, published with technical advice from the Ministry of Food following 'an increased interest in home baking and Yeast Cookery' that convinced the WI Committee that the publication would 'fill a gap in the ranks of cookery books' at that time.

Queen cakes

For a regal touch to afternoon tea, try these sweet and light queen cakes.
Quick and easy to make, they taste delicious.

Makes 10–12
Preparation time:
 15 minutes
Baking time:
 15–20 minutes

110 g (4 oz) soft **margarine**
110 g (4 oz) **caster sugar**,
 plus extra for sprinkling
2 **eggs**, beaten
110 g (4 oz) **self-raising**
 flour, sieved
a little **milk**, if necessary
60 g (2 oz) **dried fruit**

Preheat the oven to 180°C/350°F/Gas Mark 4.
Grease a 12-hole bun or mini bundt tin.

Cream the margarine and sugar together.
Add the eggs a little at a time, beating well.

Fold the flour into the mixture with a little milk,
if necessary, to give a soft dropping
consistency. Add the fruit and mix well.

Place spoonfuls of the mixture into the
prepared tin. Bake for 15–20 minutes until
firm to the touch and golden brown. Turn
out on a wire rack to cool and sprinkle with
a little extra caster sugar.

Note The recipe is taken from the *Berkshire
WI Cookery Book* (1958), a collection of
'cherished recipes', as described by Doris
Cuming in the book's foreword: 'It may be
thought that, in the future, pre-packed and
prepared food will replace the individuality of
home cooking. Although these commodities
may have to take their place in the running of
a busy home and cannot be ignored, tradition
and craft have too strong a hold on the
memory to be lost easily; by fostering good
standards of home cooking, one has some
means of comparison and discrimination.'

Variations Use 60 g (2 oz) of washed,
chopped glacé cherries instead of the dried
fruit, or replace 1 tablespoon of flour with
1 tablespoon of cocoa powder.

Bakewell tart

Hailing from the town of Bakewell in Derbyshire, this tart is as popular now as it was when it first appeared in the early 1800s.

Serves 6–8
Preparation time:
  30 minutes +
  30 minutes chilling
Baking time:
  45–50 minutes

icing sugar, for dusting

For the pastry
80 g (3 oz) **butter** or
  margarine
225 g (8 oz) **plain flour**
a pinch of **salt**
1 **egg**, beaten

For the filling
60 g (2 oz) **butter**, softened
80 g (3 oz) **caster sugar**
2 large **eggs**
80 g (3 oz) **ground almonds**
80 g (3 oz) **cake** or **bread**,
  crumbled
grated zest and juice of
  ½ **lemon**
milk, if necessary
2 tablespoons **red jam**

To make the pastry, rub the butter or margarine into the flour and salt until the mixture resembles breadcrumbs. Add the egg and enough cold water to form a dough. Wrap in cling film and chill for 30 minutes. Preheat the oven to 190°C/375°F/Gas Mark 5.

Roll out the pastry thinly on a lightly floured surface. Line an 18 cm (7 inch) pie or flan dish with the pastry, prick the base, line with non-stick baking parchment and fill with baking beans.

Bake blind for 15 minutes and then remove the baking beans and parchment and return to the oven for a further 5 minutes until dry and crisp. Remove from the oven and allow to cool. Reduce the oven temperature to 180°C/350°F/Gas Mark 4.

Cream the butter and sugar together and beat in the eggs with the ground almonds, cake or breadcrumbs and lemon zest and juice. Add a little milk if necessary to achieve the right consistency.

Spread the pastry base with the jam. Spread the almond mixture over the jam and bake for 25–30 minutes. Cool and then dust with icing sugar just before serving.

Custard tart

Wobbly baked custard and a dusting of nutmeg set in a sweet pastry crust makes this tart a true British classic.

Serves 4–6
Preparation time:
 20 minutes
Baking time:
 45 minutes

175 g (6 oz) **sweet pastry**
cornflour, for dusting
275 ml (10 fl oz) **full-fat milk**
 or **single cream**
1 large **egg**, plus 2 extra
 egg yolks
15 g (½ oz) **caster sugar**
a little grated **nutmeg**

Preheat the oven to 200°C/400°F/Gas Mark 6.

Roll out the pastry as thinly as possible on a surface dusted with cornflour. Lift the pastry on to the rolling pin and use to line an 18 cm (7 inch) loose-bottomed flan tin.

Using a little ball of pastry as a pusher, press out all the air trapped between the pastry and the tin. Prick the pastry and press again. Cover the pastry with non-stick baking parchment paper and fill with baking beans. Bake blind on a baking tray for about 15 minutes.

Meanwhile, make the custard. Bring the milk or cream to the boil and whisk the egg and egg yolks with the sugar. Slowly pour the boiling milk or cream into the egg mixture, whisking all the time. Whisk for another few minutes, by which time the flan case should be cooked. Pour the custard into a jug.

Remove the tin from the oven and remove the paper and baking beans. Lower the oven temperature to 150°C/300°F/Gas Mark 2. Replace the tin in the oven.

Pull the oven rack with the flan case a little way out of the oven and gently pour the custard into the case. Sprinkle with a little grated nutmeg. Ease the oven rack gently back into the oven and cook the tart for about 30 minutes until set.

Hereford curd cake

This is a cross between a cheesecake and a tart. Traditionally made by straining soured milk for 24 hours, this is made using natural yogurt.

Serves 8
Preparation time:
  30 minutes + draining
  + 30 minutes chilling
Baking time:
  30 minutes

For the curd
500 g (1 lb 2 oz) **natural set yogurt**
60 g (2 oz) **butter**, softened
1 **egg**, beaten
1 tablespoon **brandy**
a little grated **lemon zest**
1 tablespoon **currants**
25 g (1 oz) **caster sugar**
a pinch of **salt**
1 tablespoon **milk**
a little grated **nutmeg**

For the short pastry
60 g (2 oz) **butter** or **margarine**
140 g (5 oz) **plain flour**
a pinch of **salt**

Line a large sieve with muslin and spoon the yogurt into it. Place over a bowl and allow it to drain in the fridge for a couple of hours.

Make the pastry by rubbing the butter or margarine into the flour until the mixture resembles breadcrumbs. Add the salt and enough cold water to form a dough. Cover with cling film and chill in the fridge for 30 minutes.

Remove the curd from the muslin and mix with the butter. Add all the remaining ingredients except the grated nutmeg. Preheat the oven to 190°C/375°F/Gas Mark 5.

Roll out the pastry and use to line a 20 cm (8 inch) sandwich tin or fluted flan tin. Pour the curd mixture into the pastry case and sprinkle a little grated nutmeg over the top.

Bake for about 30 minutes until the curd mixture is set and the pastry is cooked, reducing the oven temperature to 180°C/350°F/Gas Mark 4 for the final 10 minutes.

Guernsey Gâche

Afternoon tea would be nothing on the island of Guernsey without a slab of this fruity loaf, best served toasted with lashings of Guernsey butter.

Serves 20
Preparation time:
   20 minutes + proving
Baking time:
   70–75 minutes

450 g (1 lb) **butter**, Guernsey
   if possible
675 g (1 lb 8 oz) **plain flour**
2 tablespoons **caster sugar**
4 teaspoons **fast action
   dried yeast**
a pinch of **salt**
½ teaspoon **grated nutmeg**
450 g (1 lb) **currants** or
   sultanas
110 g (4 oz) **mixed peel**
200 ml (7 fl oz) half and half
   warm **water** and **milk**

Rub the butter into the flour until the mixture resembles breadcrumbs. Add the sugar, yeast, salt, nutmeg, fruit and peel.

Make a well in the centre of the dry ingredients and gradually add enough water and milk to mix to a soft dough that leaves the bowl and your hands clean.

Knead well on an unfloured surface, place back in the bowl and cover with a thick cloth. Place in a warm place for 1½–2 hours to rise.

Preheat the oven to 180°C/350°F/Gas Mark 4. Grease a 20 cm (8 inch) deep round cake tin.

Knead the mixture again and then place in the prepared tin. Bake for 70–75 minutes until golden brown.

Fat rascals

These scones cum rock-cakes were first made in Elizabethan times. Today, a well-known Yorkshire tea room makes about 350,000 annually.

Makes 12
Preparation time:
   15 minutes + cooling
Baking time:
   12–15 minutes

110 g (4 oz) **butter**
225 g (8 oz) **self-raising flour**
a pinch of **salt**
25 g (1 oz) **caster sugar**
60 g (2 oz) **currants**
4–6 tablespoons **milk**

Preheat the oven to 190°C/375°F/Gas Mark 5. Lightly grease a baking tray.

Rub the butter into the flour and salt. Add the sugar and currants and mix with enough milk to form a soft dough.

Drop spoonfuls of the mixture on to the baking tray or roll out on a lightly floured surface to 1 cm (½ inch) thick and cut into rounds with a 5 cm (2 inch) cutter, if preferred.

Bake on the second shelf from the top for 12–15 minutes. Cool on a wire rack.

Tip If you like a sweeter cake, sprinkle with some crushed sugar lumps before baking.

Sally Lunns

Wander into any of Bath's picturesque tea shops and you'll find the Sally Lunn – a brioche-like bread traditionally served with butter or cream.

Makes 1
Preparation time:
  20 minutes + proving
Baking time:
  20 minutes

75 ml (3 fl oz) **milk**
35 g (1¼ oz) **butter**
1 **egg**, lightly beaten
450 g (1 lb) **strong plain flour**
1½ teaspoons **fast action dried yeast**
½ teaspoon **salt**
80 g (3 oz) **caster sugar**

Grease a 18 cm (7 inch) round cake tin.

Heat the milk and 150 ml (5 fl oz) of water in a small saucepan until lukewarm. Add the butter and stir to melt. Cool slightly until it is tepid. Add the egg.

Sieve the flour into a bowl. Stir in the yeast, salt and sugar. Make a well in the middle and pour in the liquid, mixing to form a soft dough.

Turn out on to a lightly floured surface and knead for about 8 minutes until smooth and elastic. Place in the prepared tin, cover and set aside in a warm place to rise for about 1 hour. Preheat the oven to 220°C/425°F/Gas Mark 7.

Bake for about 20 minutes until golden brown. Transfer to a wire rack to cool.

Dorset apple cake

From the WI Dorset Federation book – *Cookery Recipes and Household Hints* – this is still the pride of the county. Serve warm with cream.

Serves 8
Preparation time:
  15 minutes + cooling
Baking time:
  45 minutes

450 g (1 lb) **plain flour**
110 g (4 oz) **golden caster sugar**
3 teaspoons **baking powder**
225 g (8 oz) **butter**, diced
450 g (1 lb) **cooking apples**, peeled and cored
2 **eggs**, lightly beaten
60 ml (2 fl oz) **milk**

Preheat the oven to 180°C/350°F/Gas Mark 4. Grease a 23 cm (9 inch) cake tin and line with non-stick baking parchment or greased greaseproof paper.

Mix the flour, sugar and baking powder together in a large bowl. Add the butter and rub in to resemble breadcrumbs.

Grate the apples into the mixture and add the eggs and milk. Mix until combined. Spoon into the prepared tin, levelling the surface, and bake for 45 minutes until golden brown and a skewer inserted in the centre comes out clean.

Allow to cool in the tin for 10 minutes before turning out.

Tip Sprinkling the surface with demerara sugar before baking gives a lovely crunchy top.

Devonshire splits

Also known as Devonshire buns or Chudleighs, these date back to the 19th century and are traditionally served with treacle or jam and clotted cream.

Makes 16
Preparation time:
20 minutes + rising
Baking time:
15–20 minutes

450 g (1 lb) **plain flour**
½ teaspoon **salt**
1 teaspoon **caster sugar**
7 g sachet **fast action dried yeast**
300 ml (10 fl oz) warm **skimmed milk**
60 g (2 oz) **butter**, melted

Syrup
110 g (4 oz) **caster sugar**
75 ml (3 fl oz) **milk**

To serve
jam
clotted cream
icing sugar, sifted

Grease and flour two baking trays. Sift the flour and salt into a mixing bowl and stir in the sugar and yeast. Add the milk and melted butter and mix to form a soft dough.

Turn out on to a lightly floured surface and knead for 10 minutes. Put into a floured bowl, cover with a clean damp tea towel or oiled cling film and set aside in a warm place until doubled in size (about 30 minutes). Preheat the oven to 200°C/400°F/Gas Mark 6.

Turn out the dough and divide into 16 equal portions. Knead into small balls with the palm of the hand. Place on the prepared baking trays, cover with a tea towel and set aside for 10–15 minutes or until doubled in size. Bake for 15–20 minutes until golden brown.

Heat the sugar and milk together until the sugar has dissolved and brush the hot cooked buns with this syrupy mixture to make them soft and sticky.

When cold, split, fill with jam and Devonshire clotted cream and dust with a little icing sugar.

Lincolnshire plum bun

Plum is an old English word for mixed fruit. This is a delicious moist tea loaf, ideally served cut into thin slices and buttered.

Makes 2 x 2 lb loaves or 1 x 2 lb loaf + 6 mini loaves
Preparation time: 20 minutes
Baking time: 50 minutes–1½ hours

150 g (5½ oz) **butter** or **margarine**, softened
300 g (10½ oz) **light muscovado sugar**
1 **egg**, lightly beaten
1 tablespoon **rum** (optional)
450 g (1 lb) **self-raising flour**
1 teaspoon **mixed spice**
250 g (9 oz) **currants**
250 g (9 oz) **sultanas**
40 g (1½ oz) chopped **mixed peel**
40 g (1½ oz) **glacé cherries**
150 ml (5 fl oz) **milk** or **cold tea**

Preheat the oven to 150°C/300°F/Gas Mark 2. Grease two 900 g (2 lb) loaf tins and line with non-stick baking parchment or greased greaseproof paper. Alternatively, prepare one 900 g (2 lb) tin and six mini 200 ml (7 fl oz) loaf tins.

Cream the butter or margarine and sugar together and mix in the egg and rum, if using.

Fold in the flour and then the remaining ingredients.

Divide the mixture between the prepared tins and bake for 1¼–1½ hours for the larger tins and 50–60 minutes for the mini ones. They are done when they are golden brown and a skewer inserted into the centre comes out clean.

Tip This will keep for up to a fortnight in an airtight tin.

Wiltshire lardy cake

Enriched with sugar and spices and studded with fruit, this rich and gooey tea bread is not for the faint-hearted. Best enjoyed warm with a cup of tea.

Serves 8–10
Preparation time:
30 minutes + rising
Baking time:
25–30 minutes

450 g (1 lb) **strong white bread flour**
½ teaspoon **salt**
½ teaspoon **mixed spice**
1½ teaspoons **fast action dried yeast**
110 g (4 oz) **caster sugar**
300 ml (10 fl oz) warm **milk**

To finish
110 g (4 oz) **lard** or **white vegetable fat**
110 g (4 oz) **caster sugar**, plus 2 tablespoons for topping
110 g (4 oz) mixed **dried fruit**

Warm the flour, salt and spice by heating it in the microwave for a few seconds or popping it into a warm oven for a few minutes.

Stir in the yeast and sugar and then gradually add enough warm milk to mix to a soft but not sticky dough.

Knead well on a lightly floured surface for about 10 minutes until the dough is smooth and elastic. Place in a clean bowl and cover with a damp tea towel or greased cling film. Set aside in a warm place until doubled in size – about 1 hour.

Knead the dough again for a few minutes and then roll out on a well floured board to a rectangle about 4 mm (¼ inch) thick. Spread on half the lard, sugar and fruit. Fold in three, folding the bottom third up and the top third down, turn the mixture 90 degrees to the left and roll out again. Cover with the rest of the lard, sugar and fruit and fold in three again.

Roll out to a 2.5 cm (1 inch) thick oblong that will fit in a greased 25 x 20 cm (10 x 8 inch) roasting tin. Place the dough in the tin, cover with greased cling film and stand in a warm place until well risen (30–45 minutes). Preheat the oven to 220°C/425°F/Gas Mark 7.

Score the top of the dough in a criss-cross pattern with a knife. Dissolve the remaining 2 tablespoons of sugar in 2 tablespoons of hot water and brush the top of the cake.

Bake for 25–30 minutes until well risen and golden brown. Check after 20 minutes and cover loosely with foil if the top seems to be browning too much.

Tips The lard can be replaced with butter for a healthier version.

Rather than brushing the cake with a sugar solution before baking, you could just sprinkle the sugar over the top of the cake when it comes out of the oven.

Biscuits
and bakes

Chocolate caramel slices

Traditional biscuit bases covered with gooey delicious caramel and topped with melted chocolate. Rich but fabulous.

Makes 18
Preparation time:
30 minutes + cooling
Baking time:
25 minutes

For the base
110 g (4 oz) **butter** or
 margarine
140 g (5 oz) **plain flour**
a pinch of **salt**
60 g (2 oz) **caster sugar**

Filling
110 g (4 oz) **margarine**
2 tablespoons **golden syrup**
110 g (4 oz) **light brown soft**
 sugar
1 small tin **condensed milk**
a few drops of **vanilla**
 extract

Topping
110 g (4 oz) **plain chocolate**
 (70% cocoa solids),
 broken into pieces

Preheat the oven to 160°C/325°F/Gas Mark 3. Grease an 18 cm (7 inch) square loose-bottomed tin.

For the base, rub the butter or margarine into the flour, salt and sugar. Knead into a ball and then press out evenly into the prepared tin. Bake for 25 minutes. Leave to cool before adding the filling and topping.

For the filling, slowly melt the margarine, syrup, sugar and condensed milk together, stirring continuously. Bring to the boil and, still stirring, simmer gently for exactly 7 minutes.

Add the vanilla extract, pour on to the base and leave to cool.

For the topping, melt the chocolate gently in a bowl over a pan of simmering water. Beat until it is smooth.

Spread the chocolate evenly over the filling. When set, cut into nine squares and then cut each square in half again to make 18 slices.

Tips If you don't have a loose-bottomed tin, line the tin with non-stick baking parchment, snipping into the corners of the paper so it lines the bottom and sides. This makes it easier to remove the slices.

It is easier to cut this into slices if you make it the day before and chill in the fridge.

Butterfly cakes

An old-fashioned favourite loved by all and fun to make with children. Decorate with ready-made icing and sweets to take into school fêtes.

Makes 12
Preparation time:
  30 minutes + cooling
Cooking time:
  15–18 minutes

110 g (4 oz) soft **margarine**
110 g (4 oz) **caster sugar**
110 g (4 oz) **self-raising flour**
½ teaspoon **baking powder**
2 **eggs**
1 teaspoon **vanilla essence**

Butter cream frosting
110 g (4 oz) **butter**, softened
225 g (8 oz) **icing sugar**,
  sifted, plus extra to
  decorate
½ teaspoon **vanilla essence**
1–2 teaspoons **milk**

Preheat the oven to 180°C/350°F/Gas Mark 4. Line a 12-hole bun tin with paper cake cases.

Place the margarine, sugar, flour and baking powder in a mixing bowl, add the eggs and vanilla essence and beat until smooth with a wooden spoon or electric mixer.

Spoon into the cake cases, level the tops and bake for 15–18 minutes until well risen and golden brown and the tops spring back when pressed lightly with a fingertip. Leave the cakes to cool a little in the tin then transfer to a wire rack.

To make the frosting, beat the butter and half the icing sugar in a bowl until smooth. Add the remaining icing sugar and the vanilla essence and beat until soft and smooth, adding milk as needed.

Cut a small circle from the top of each cake using a teaspoon. Pipe or spoon butter cream into the centre of the cakes. Cut the small cake circles in half and press into the butter cream at angles to resemble wings. Dust lightly with a little extra sifted icing sugar.

Macaroons

This recipe for old-fashioned flat macaroons is taken from the *WI Book of Party Recipes* (1969).

Makes 16
Preparation time:
  10 minutes + cooling
Baking time:
  about 20 minutes

rice paper
3 **egg whites**
110 g (4 oz) **ground almonds**
25 g (1 oz) **ground rice**
225 g (8 oz) **caster sugar**
16 **blanched almonds**

Preheat the oven to 150°C/300°F/Gas Mark 2. Line two baking trays with rice paper.

Whisk 2 egg whites in a clean bowl until they form stiff peaks. Fold in the ground almonds, ground rice and caster sugar. Place 16 small heaps of the mixture on the prepared trays, spacing them out so that there is room for them to spread.

Top each macaroon with an almond and glaze the whole macaroons very lightly with a little of the remaining egg white. Bake for about 20 minutes until they are pale golden brown.

Allow to cool for a few minutes and then transfer to a wire rack. Carefully remove the excess rice paper.

Tip Non-stick baking parchment can be used if you cannot find rice paper.

Chocolate brownies

The addition of white chocolate and walnuts makes these brownies a little bit special. They are best served warm, ideally with real vanilla ice cream.

Makes 20–24
Preparation time:
20 minutes + cooling
Baking time:
30 minutes

110 g (4 oz) **butter**, diced
110 g (4 oz) **plain chocolate**
(70% cocoa solids),
broken into pieces
1 tablespoon **golden syrup**
140 g (5 oz) **dark muscovado sugar**
140 g (5 oz) **caster sugar**
4 **eggs**, beaten
225 g (8 oz) **self-raising flour**
40 g (1½ oz) **cocoa powder**
60 g (2 oz) **white chocolate**,
broken into small pieces
60 g (2 oz) **walnut pieces**

Preheat the oven to 180°C/350°F/Gas Mark 4. Line the base and sides of a 30 × 22 cm (12 × 9 inch) Swiss roll tin with non-stick baking parchment or greased greaseproof paper.

Place the butter, plain chocolate and syrup in a large saucepan and melt together over a gentle heat.

Remove from the heat, add all the other ingredients and mix together thoroughly. Spoon the mixture into the prepared tin and spread evenly into the corners.

Bake for about 30 minutes until risen, firm to the touch and coming away from the sides of the tin. Allow to cool in the tin. When cold, cut into squares to serve.

Éclairs

Everyone's favourite – light, crisp pastry fingers filled with cream and iced with chocolate.

Makes 12
Preparation time:
 45 minutes + cooling
Baking time:
 30–35 minutes

275 ml (10 fl oz) **whipping cream**
25 g (1 oz) **icing sugar**
75 g (2¾ oz) **plain chocolate** (70% cocoa solids), broken into pieces
15 g (½ oz) **butter**
60 g (2 oz) **icing sugar**, sifted

Choux pastry
60 g (2 oz) **butter**, diced
70 g (2½ oz) **strong white flour**
1 teaspoon **caster sugar**
2 **eggs**, beaten

Preheat the oven to 200°C/400°F/Gas Mark 6. Arrange two shelves in the top half of the oven if it isn't fan assisted. Grease and flour two baking trays.

To make the choux pastry, put 150 ml (5 fl oz) of cold water and the butter in a saucepan. Place over a medium heat until the butter has melted and it all comes to the boil. Meanwhile, sieve the flour on to a sheet of baking parchment that has been folded in half.

Remove the butter water from the heat and 'shoot' the flour into the mixture with the sugar. Beat vigorously with a wooden spoon (or use an electric hand whisk) until you have a smooth ball of paste.

Add the eggs gradually, beating well between each addition until the paste is smooth and glossy. Spoon the mixture into a piping bag with a 1 cm (½ inch) plain nozzle and pipe 9 cm (3½ inch) lengths of pastry diagonally on to the baking trays, leaving plenty of room between them.

Bake for 20 minutes until well risen and then reduce the temperature to 160°C/320°F/Gas Mark 3. Cook for a further 5–10 minutes until crisp. Make a small slit in the side of each éclair to let the steam escape and return to the oven for a few minutes to dry out the centres. Cool on a wire rack.

Whip the cream and icing sugar together. When the éclairs have cooled, extend the slit and fill with the sweetened cream.

For the chocolate icing, melt the chocolate in a bowl over a pan of hot (but not boiling) water. Stir in the butter until melted and then add the icing sugar and 1–2 tablespoons of hot water to form a smooth glossy icing. Cover the top of each éclair with icing and leave to set.

Coconut slices

These traditional favourites are sweet, moist and perfect for tea parties. On a cold day, eat warm with home-made custard.

Makes 21
Preparation time:
  20 minutes + cooling
Baking time:
  25–30 minutes

110 g (4 oz) soft **margarine**
110 g (4 oz) **caster sugar**
3 **egg yolks**
225 g (8 oz) **self-raising flour**
5 tablespoons **raspberry jam**

Topping
3 **egg whites**
85 g (3 oz) **caster sugar**
140 g (5 oz) **desiccated coconut**

Preheat the oven to 180°C/350°F/Gas Mark 4. Grease a 30 x 20 cm (12 x 8 inch) Swiss roll tin.

Cream the margarine and sugar together and add the egg yolks and flour slowly to make a very stiff mixture.

Pour the mixture into the prepared tin and spread it out evenly, right to the corners. Spread with the raspberry jam.

Whisk the egg whites in a clean bowl until stiff peaks form and then add the sugar and coconut. Whisk again until the sugar has dissolved.

Spread this mixture on top of the jam and bake for 25–30 minutes until the meringue is golden. Leave to cool and then cut into slices.

Strawberry shortcakes

Old-fashioned favourites consisting of fresh strawberries and cream sandwiched between melt-in-the-mouth shortcake biscuits.

Makes 6
Preparation time:
  40 minutes + cooling
Baking time:
  8–10 minutes

225 g (8 oz) **self-raising flour**
a pinch of **salt**
25 g (1 oz) **ground almonds**
125 g (4½ oz) **butter**
60 g (2 oz) **caster sugar**, plus
  extra for sprinkling
1 **egg yolk**

To decorate
150 ml (10 fl oz) **double
  cream**
1 tablespoon **caster sugar**
250 g (9 oz) **strawberries**,
  3 reserved and the
  remainder sliced

Preheat the oven to 180°C/350°F/Gas Mark 4. Lightly grease a baking tray.

Sift the flour and salt together and mix in the ground almonds.

Cream the butter and sugar together and add the egg yolk. Work in the flour and almond mixture using your fingers to make a fine dough.

Roll the mixture out on a lightly floured surface to about 4 mm (¼ inch) thick and cut out 12 x 7 cm (2¾ inch) rounds using a fluted cutter and re-rolling as needed.

Place on the prepared tray, sprinkle with a little caster sugar and bake for 8–10 minutes. Leave to go cold.

Whip the cream, adding the sugar, and pipe a rosette on top of six of the biscuits.

Fold the sliced strawberries into the remaining cream and spoon on top of the remaining biscuits. Add the rosette-topped biscuits and decorate each with half a strawberry.

Afternoon tea biscuits

Variations of the afternoon tea biscuit feature in many of the WI recipe books of the past century. These are light and sweet with a lemony topping.

Makes 12
Preparation time:
  15 minutes
Baking time:
  15–20 minutes

80 g (3 oz) **butter**, softened
60 g (2 oz) **caster sugar**
1 **egg**, beaten
175 g (6 oz) **plain flour**
raspberry jam

Lemon icing
110 g (4 oz) **icing sugar**
lemon juice

Preheat the oven to 180°C/350°F/Gas Mark 4. Lightly grease a baking tray.

Cream the butter and sugar together and beat in three-quarters of the egg with 1 tablespoon of the flour. Add the remainder of the flour and, if necessary, the remaining egg.

Mix to a stiff paste and roll out on a lightly floured surface to about 5 mm (¼ inch) thick. Cut into 12 rounds using a 6 cm (2½ inch) cutter and re-rolling as needed.

Place on the prepared baking tray and bake for 15–20 minutes until golden brown.

While hot, coat half the biscuits with jam and sandwich the jam-coated and plain biscuits together in pairs.

To make the icing, sieve the icing sugar into a bowl and mix with lemon juice until you get the right consistency. Decorate the biscuits.

Shortbread

Traditionally associated with Scotland, classic shortbread is perfect for a vintage afternoon tea wherever you are.

Makes 10–12
Preparation time:
15 minutes + cooling
Baking time:
25–30 minutes

110 g (4 oz) **butter**
60 g (2 oz) **caster sugar**
140 g (5 oz) **plain flour**
80 g (3 oz) **rice flour**

Preheat the oven to 160°C/320°F/Gas Mark 3. Lightly grease two baking trays.

Cream the butter and sugar together and gradually add the flours.

Roll out on a floured surface into two 1 cm (½ inch) thick rounds. Place on the prepared baking trays.

Mark each round into triangles and bake for 25–30 minutes.

Allow to cool a little before lifting the shortbread off the baking trays on to a wire rack.

Variations For traditional variations, try one of the following.

Pitcaithly Bannock – Add 1 tablespoon of chopped peel and 1 tablespoon of chopped almonds.

Huby Bannock – Add 1 tablespoon of chopped preserved ginger and 1 tablespoon of chopped almonds.

Gingerbread

Based on a secret gingerbread recipe from the Lake District, this WI version of the classic makes a perfect gift.

Serves 12
Preparation time:
15 minutes + cooling
Baking time:
45 minutes

450 g (1 lb) **plain flour**
225 g (8 oz) **light brown soft sugar**, plus extra for sprinkling
2 teaspoons **ground ginger**
1 teaspoon **bicarbonate of soda**
1 teaspoon **cream of tartar**
225 g (8 oz) **margarine** or **butter**

Preheat the oven to 150°C/300°F/Gas Mark 2. Lightly grease a 30 x 25 cm (12 x 10 inch) tin.

Mix together the dry ingredients and then rub in the margarine or butter. Press the mixture into the prepared tin.

Bake for about 45 minutes. Mark into 12 bars when it comes out of the oven and sprinkle with a little extra sugar. Allow the gingerbread to cool slightly before cutting it into pieces.

Note This was first made by domestic servant Sarah Nelson in 1854. Wrap in waxed paper or non-stick baking parchment and tie with fine ribbon or string for a charming parcel.

Ginger crunchies

This name is very apt as these lightly spiced crunchy biscuits are very moreish and a perfect accompaniment to a really good cup of tea.

Makes 16
Preparation time:
  20 minutes + cooling
Baking time:
  15–20 minutes

110 g (4 oz) **butter**, softened
60 g (2 oz) **caster sugar**
140 g (5 oz) **plain flour**
1 teaspoon **baking powder**
1 teaspoon **ground ginger**
stem ginger (optional)

Topping
4 tablespoons **icing sugar**
2 tablespoons **butter**
1 teaspoon **ground ginger**
3 teaspoons **golden syrup**

Preheat the oven to 180°C/350°F/Gas Mark 4. Line a 20 cm (8 inch) square tin with foil (this makes it easier to lift the biscuits out).

Cream the butter and sugar together in a bowl. Add the flour, baking powder and ground ginger and mix well.

Press into the prepared tin and bake for 15–20 minutes.

For the topping, place all the ingredients into a small saucepan and stir over a gentle heat until mixed. Pour over the biscuit layer while still warm and cut into squares. Decorate each square with a little stem ginger, if using. Leave until cold to lift out.

Index